MARTHA OSPINA

Pergamano®
PAINTING
ON
PARCHMENT

LA RIVIÈRE
CREATIEVE UITGEVERS

Pergamano® is the brand name under which books, materials and tools for the creative hobby Parchment Craft are marketed. Pergamano® is a registered brand name.

© 1998 La Rivière, creatieve uitgevers, Baarn

ISBN 90 384 1300 9
NUGI 440

Photography: De studio - fotografie+digitale beeldbewerking, Utrecht
Typesetting: Studio Imago, Amersfoort
Printing: Van der Weij bv grafische bedrijven, Hilversum

INDEX

PREVIEW

I am sure many people have been looking forward to this book on the basic techniques of Painting on Parchment paper. Through Parchment Craft you are bound to be introduced to "the paint brush". This idea might scare people off and make them think: I can't draw, let alone paint, so no, this is not for me. But, on the contrary, Parchment Craft will help people overcome their initial concerns. One only has to trace a pattern on the parchment paper, you do not have to be an artist or be able to draw to be able to paint on parchment paper, and this is one of the biggest "pluses" of this hobby!

This book came into being with the help of two Registered Pergamano tutors: Randi Hanson of Denmark and Gerti Hofman of the Netherlands. Randi had already won her spurs with porcelain painting, but when she discovered Parchment Craft, she immediately got "hooked".

Gerti, originally an illustrator, helped me with the chapter on the theory of colour.

I would like to thank both ladies very much for their help.

I hope that for some this book will be the last necessary push in the direction of painting, and for others an easy-reference manual to Painting on Parchment.

I wish you many pleasant hours of painting

Martha Ospina

INTRODUCTION

Painting is the most important technique in Parchment Craft, and it will probably be also the last technique you learn. After all, you first have to learn how to trace from a pattern, emboss, perforate and cut. If you have just started Parchment Craft and have not yet learned these basic techniques, or have not yet mastered them properly, I suggest you first buy the book Pergamano Basic techniques (ISBN 90 384 1247 9). This book teaches the above-mentioned techniques, as well as the techniques of stippling, dorsing, working with the Easy-Grid template and colouring with the Perga-Liner pencils (dry technique).

The attractive side of painting is that it is not easy to do. You might find this a strange thing to say, but I will explain. Often, the interest in a hobby will fade once people fully master the necessary technique(s). Painting however, is something that will always keep you interested, as you will always see something that you could paint better or more beautifully: the challenge remains.

Furthermore, painting with a brush on parchment paper is something anyone can do, as it does not involve painting like Rembrandt or Van Gogh, two famous Dutch painters. We are talking about the colouring of a traced pattern with paint and a brush, which of course is much easier to do than first having to draw your own pattern on canvas or paper. The remainder though is just like real painting: we use delicate sable brushes, waterproof inks and acrylic paints (which are actually easier to work with than oil paint).

In this book you will learn how to use your brush, how to mix colours, how to put the paint on your brush, how to apply the paint and how to make shades, an important aspect of painting on parchment paper.

With the explanations in this book you will be able to teach yourself painting on parchment paper. The many step-by-step pictures and detailed instructions will be of great help. Should you require more help, you can attend a course run by from a Registered Pergamano Tutor. Following a course is not only very interesting and helpful, it is also great fun. You will learn the tricks of the trade, get useful tips and at the same time meet people with the same hobby and the same little technical problems. You are cannot avoid making new friends on such a course!

Lots of success!

PERGAMANO MATERIALS

Parchment paper:
Pergamano paper A4 (code 1481)

Embossing tools:
Fine stylus (code 1103)
Extra fine (code 1107)
Small ball (code 1101)
Large ball (code 1102)
Hockey Stick (code 1100)

Perforation tools:
1-needle (code 1104)
2-needle (code 1106)
3-needle (code 1108)
4-needle (code 1105)
5-needle (code 1112)
7-needle - flower tool (code 1111)

Pads:
Felt embossing pad (code 1410)
Perforation pad, excellent (code 1419)
Embossing pad, De lux (code 1413)

Paints:
Tinta ink
Pintura paint
Pinta-Perla paint
Perga-Color (code 1430)
Perga-Liners Box I (code 1451)
Dorso crayons Box I (code 1440)
Dorso crayons Box II (code 1442)

Miscellaneous:
Mapping pen (code 1420)
Perga-Soft (code 1802)
Paint/ink eraser (code 1423)
White pencil (code 9202)
Perga-Stamp, PS-1 (code 1821)
Stamping pad
Silver Embossing powder

Brushes

Introduction to the Pergamano brushes:

▶ Brush no. 2, light brown: This brush is especially made for the children's programme, where the painting is done in conjuntion with the Perga-Colors.
▶ Brush no. 0 and no. 2, Marten-hair: These soft haired brushes are used for applying Tinta ink, Pintura and Pinta-Perla paints, and they offer excellent painting results.
▶ Brush no. 2, Kolinsky: An artists quality brush with high quality hair that gives the brush bounce. This brush is used for applying the Perga-Liners, but can also improve the application of the Tinta ink, Pintura and Pinta-Perla paints.

How to treat the brush:
Brushes should always be handled with care, whether painting or cleaning. Mishandling can ruin your brush as the hairs are very easily damaged.

How to fill the brush:
There are many ways of loading the brush, but in whatever way it should be done carefully. Never press the hairs down hard on to the palette. Always try to hold the brush in a horizontal position when loaded with the paint.

How to clean the brush:
Tap water is used for cleaning the brushes. Use a tall container (approx. 100 - 250ml), and with a large amount of water the particles from the paints are able to sink to the bottom, therefore leaving the surface water clean.
When cleaning the brush, the hairs are dipped into the water and moved from side to side so that the hairs spread and the paint rinsed out. If the paint holds the bristles together, the tip of the brush can gently be pushed towards the side of the container in order to spread the hairs a little.
N.B. Never press the brush on the bottom of the container or leave the brush standing in the water container as this will ruin your brush.
After cleaning, the brush should always be made to retain its point by gently pressing it against some kitchen paper or a damp Pergamano sponge.

Upkeep of the brush:

The brush must always be kept in a way to preserve the hairs. In practice this means that nothing should touch the hairs whilst it is stored.

When new, the brush tip is protected by a plastic tube. You might like to keep this tube for further protection, but before placing the tube on the brush, the hairs have to be cleaned in water and shaped into a point before carefully placing the tube over the hairs. Do be careful that no hairs bend back as this may ruin your brush.

Divided hairs:

If the brush is damaged the hairs will spread out to all sides and it is impossible to reshape the hairs again into a nice point.

The brush can also split if it is not adequately loaded with paint. It takes a certain quantity of moisture/paint to bind the hairs together, so if you only want to have a little paint on the tip of the brush, the hairs must contain enough water to keep them together.

Pergamano sponge

When practising the Pintura and Pinta-Perla techniques the sponge can be used to drain the brush after it has been cleaned in water. When new, the sponge has a thickness of 3 mm, but swells to 26mm when soaked with water. This thickness will not change anymore, even when the sponge has dried.

Container for water

For cleaning the brush a tall container is needed, (capacity 100 - 250 ml.)

Two white saucers

One to place the wet Pergamano sponge on, when painting with Pintura and Pinta-Perla paints.

The other to use as a palette when painting.

Other materials

For the process of making cards other materials are needed:

Tape, scissors for cutting paper, kitchen paper, ruler, a piece of cardboard, hobby knife, cutting mat, paper clips, sewing needle, thin gold or sewing thread, different colours of thin paper (80 g) for inserts, nylon stocking, plastic stirrer.

THEORY OF COLOUR

It is important that you know something about the theory of colour when you start painting. The actual technique of painting is very important, but it is also quite important to know a little bit about the meaning of a colour or the combination of different colours. You obtain a much better composition when you have the right colour balance.

The origin of colour
We need light to be able to see colours, and the most important source of light is sunlight. It is made up of a combination of various colours that reach us as a white (colourless) light.

In 1676 the scientist Isaac Newton was able to show that the white sunlight can be split in to a prism of colours (see picture). Because every colour in a ray of sunlight has its own angle of refraction they then come out of a prism separately. The rays are refracted twice: first upon entering and then upon leaving the prism. This creates a colour range which the human eye is able to see, showing the colours red, orange, yellow, green, blue and violet.
We know of many sorts of light, and the different effects they give. When we are enjoying a beautiful landscape, the colours we see in the evening will be quite different from the colours we see during the day. Different types of artificial light also give different effects, think of the difference between a table lamp, fluorescent light or candlelight.

Mixing
Tinta inks and Pintura paints are available in many colours, but it can still be very handy to be able to mix your own colours; not just to be able to make the colours that you are unable to buy, but because it is great fun to discover how you can create a large variety of colours, and therefore effects, with just a few basic colours. If you want to make a particular colour without knowing which colours are required, the result can be very disappointing. If you then keep on adding colours in your search for the desired colour, you will most probably end up with an ugly greyish colour.

Primary colours
Primary colours are also known as basic colours. They are so pure that they cannot be obtained through the mixing of other colours, whereas all other non-primary colours can be obtained by mixing. The primary colours are red, yellow and blue. By mixing these three basic colours, you can, in principle, create any other colour you desire.

Secondary colours
Secondary colours are colours that can be obtained by mixing two primary colours. Red and yellow will result in orange, blue and red will result in violet (purple), and yellow and blue will result in green. The mix is very important; if you take a lot of red and just a little bit of yellow, you will not create a true orange, but more a sort of reddy-orange. Through practise you will be able to create a large variety of colours and with experience you will become more skilful in knowing the right colour quantities to use.

Tertiary colours
Tertiary colours are colours that can be obtained by mixing a primary colour with a secondary colour:
Yellow and orange = orange-yellow
Red   and orange = orange-red
Red   and violet = violet-red
Blue   and violet = violet-blue
Blue   and green = green-blue
Yellow and green = green-yellow

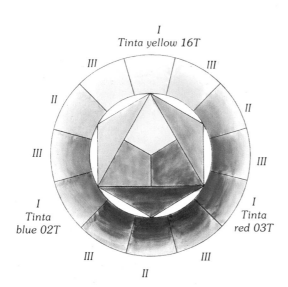

Colour circle with Tinta inks.

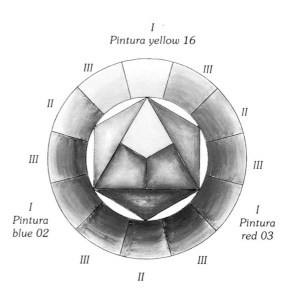

Colour circle with Pintura paints.

The Colour circle

The best way to become familiar with the colour circle is to make your own circle with Pergamano Tinta ink or Pintura paint. By doing this you will learn to mix new colours from the three primary colours. You will also be able to see the effect of shading by painting every separate little area of the circle darker on the inside and lighter on the outside.

In the pictures you see colour circles painted with Tinta ink and with Pintura paint. You can see the three primary colours (I) in the inner triangle. In the flat triangles against the inner triangles you can see the secondary colours (II). These primary and secondary colours are repeated in the circle. Tertiary colours (III) are made by mixing primary and secondary colours.

Complementary colours

Complementary colours are also called opposite colours; you will find them opposite each other in the colour circle. If you put them next to each other, you will have a strong contrast in colours: for example yellow opposite purple, red opposite green and blue opposite orange (see picture).

Cold-warm contrast

If you look at a landscape through a yellow filter it will appear warm and sunny, if you look at the same landscape through a blue filter, it will appear cold and chilly. This is a clear example of the cold-warm contrast. The colours yellow, orange-yellow, orange, orange-red, red and violet-red are warm colours. Yellow-green, green, blue-green, blue, violet-blue and violet are cold colours.

Green and violet could also be called intermediate colours. If you paint green next to yellow, it will appear much colder than when you would paint green next to blue. If you paint violet next to blue, it will appear much warmer than when you would paint violet next to red. Trials have shown that people began to feel cold in a blue room at a temperature of about 15 degrees Celsius, whereas they began to feel cold in an orange-red room only at a temperature of about 11-12 degrees Celsius.

Colour and mood

Certain feelings and themes can make you think of certain colours. Try this out for yourself while thinking of the following (or other) themes: Anger, aggression (red, black, brown), Love (pink, light yellow, light blue), Sadness (grey, dark violet), Winter (white, light blue, blue-grey) Noise (red), Spring (yellow, light green).

Harmony of colours

Harmony means that there is a unity that is not disrupted anywhere. Harmony of colours is often a matter of personal taste, and you may find that your taste may change with age.

Sources: LOI, NTI, Theory of Colour by J. Itten.

TINTA INK

Tinta inks are water-soluble as long as they are kept wet, but when they dry out they become waterproof. There are three kinds of Tinta inks: Metallic, white and transparent.

Metallic inks (gold/silver):
The metallic inks are silver and gold. Because the metallic colour is heavy, it quickly sinks to the bottom of the bottle. It is therefore necessary to stir the gold/silver with a thin stick. To ensure a good colour mix, give the pot a good stir with the stick and you then use the paint adhereing to the stick to put on to the brush. It is not necessary to actually put the brush into the pot, as normally sufficient paint will have been left on the stick. It normally takes two coats of gold or silver to give the necessary depth of colour.

White ink:
The white ink is a matt opaque colour. When used, it is normally thinned with water, so it will appear a little more transparent. The bottle has to be shaken before use.

Transparent inks:
The transparent inks are available in 10 different colours. A thin coat of transparent ink appears matt, but several coats of colour gives a slight sheen to the surface.

Painting with the Tinta inks:
The inks have a very thin consistency, so a dry brush is used for painting.
A little drop of ink is placed on the palette before the brush can be filled. Do not load the brush by dipping it into the ink bottle, as the brush will be too wet and will therefore makre the parchment crinkle. The surface of the paper can only obtain a small quantity of colour/water and it is therefore important only to have small amounts of ink on the brush.
If a stronger colour is needed, it can be achieved by applying many separate coats, each applied only when the previous coat is completely dry.
The inks may be mixed in numerous ways, enabling you to create your own colours.

Technique: Painting with a flat brush
The most simple form of painting with Tinta ink is to fill out traced spaces with a thin coat of colour. To make these areas as smooth as possible the painting is done with a flat brush.
How to fill the brush.
Place a drop of ink on the palette. Place the point of a clean dry brush in the outer edge of the drop. Move the brush gently from side to side, so the hairs spread out a little. Now and then role the brush and repeat the side to side movement. The brush is held in as horizontal a position as possible, so the hairs are straight. If the brush is held too vertically, the hairs may break.
If a large area is to be painted, the brush can be fully loaded with paint (from the point to the bottom of the brush). If a small area is to be painted, only the tip of the brush should be loaded. So adjust the loading of the brush to the required area to be painted.
Leave the brush flat after it is loaded with ink.

How to hold the brush:
Hold the brush above the metal where the wooden handle begins.

Position of the brush:
During the work the brush is held at an angle of 45 to 90 degrees.

The brush movement:
Place the flat brush on the paper and pull the brush towards you. Keep the pressure constant so the hairs continue to be spread. Lift the brush up quickly.

Wide areas:
If the area is wider than can be covered with one stroke of the brush, more brushstrokes can be added. If you are right handed, you start painting from the left side. While the first brushstroke is still wet a new one is painted on top of the right side of the first brushstroke. Continue this process until the whole area is covered.
If you paint with the left hand you start painting in the right side of the area.

Tips:

If the brush is too full, the brush will leave a small drop of paint when the brush is lifted. If this happens immediately remove the excess paint with a dry brush.

Place the traced design on a piece of white paper. It makes it easier to follow the pattern.

Example A: Butterflies

Tracing:

Tinta sepia 12T: The butterflies.

Tinta gold 22T: The curved outline and the drop shaped figures.

White colour pencil: The straight outlines.

Remove the Pergamano paper from the design and place it on a piece of white paper.

Colour guide for painting:

Tinta blue 02T: Pattern in the wings.

Tinta fuchsia 20T: Pattern in the wings.

Tinta yellow 16T: The small spots close to the body.

Mix Tinta sepia 12T and Tinta violet 07T: The body and the ground colour of the wings.

Painting instructions:

1: Use Tinta blue to paint (on the front side) the 5 small spots in all the top wings. Use a flat brush to paint strokes in the natural direction of the wing, going from the outside towards the body. Paint the two oblong figures close to the body of the largest butterfly. Start in the left side of the area and place the brushstrokes close together to make a even finish. Sometimes thin dark stripes appears, but it is OK as long as the lines follow the natural direction of the wing. Finally paint the centre figure of the lower wings.

2: When the blue ink is dry, paint a second coat on all blue parts, still following the natural direction of the wings.

3: Use Tinta fuchsia to paint the large area in the top wings. Continue painting from the outside towards the body. Be careful on the large butterfly to avoid over painting the blue area. Let the first coat of fuchsia is dry before applying the second coat.

Paint a little Tinta yellow in the two small spots by the lower wings. Only load the brush with a very little yellow.

4. For the rest of the butterflies a new colour is mixed. Place two drops of Tinta sepia and one drop of Tinta violet on to the palette. Mix the colours together with a clean brush. Paint the bodies and the rest of the wings with a thin coat of the mixed colour.

At this stage the butterflies will appear rather flat. They need some shadows. The shadows are also painted with the colour mixed of sepia and violet. Make a thin line along the outer edge of the body and of the wings. Here the brush should not be too loaded or too flat. When shading, the tip of the brush should just touch the traced outline. The shaded area must appear a little darker than the first coat. If the butterflies need a darker shadow in some places, a second coat of shading colour can be added. Also give the yellow parts of the wing a thin wash of colour to take it down in brightness. Without the shading, the yellow colour is too strong.

Dorsing:

Using Dorso lilac (ass. 2):

Dorso the lower part of the card and spread the colour evenly towards the centre.

Using Dorso blue (ass. 1): colour the central area and blend towards the top of the card.

Using Dorso light blue (ass. 2): colour the top part of the card.

Embossing:

Place the card on the design again. On the front side emboss the thin lines with the extra fine ball tool. Use a ruler to support the embossing.

Perforating:

Perforate the four-hole combinations gently with the 4-needle.

Embossing:

Emboss the blue, fuchsia and yellow part of the wings. In the larger areas the embossing is done with a "press and lift movement" going towards

the body. The embossing is first done with the large ball, and more effect is then later made with the small ball. Finally, the bodies of the butterflies should be embossed with the large ball tool.

The drop shaped figures are embossed with the small ball. On the inner side of the gold outline a thin white line is embossed with the extra fine ball tool.

Cutting:
Fully perforate, then cut the perforations into crosses.

Finishing off:
Fold the card and insert a coloured paper of your own choice. Perforate along the curved outline with the two-needle tool. Cut the rest of the outlines with a hobby knife and ruler. Remove the excess paper.

PATTERN A: BUTTERFLIES

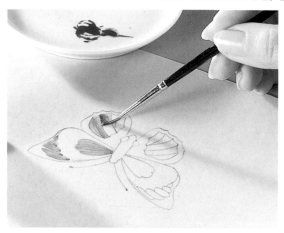

1. *Applying the first layer of Tinta blue.*

2. *Applying the second layer of Tinta blue.*

3. *Finished with fuchsia and yellow.*

4. *Applying shadowlines with Tinta sepia + violet.*

5. *Embossed at the back.*

Technique: Dabbing

To illustrate small thin petals i.e. as on a daisy, Tinta ink is dabbed onto the paper. The brush is loaded with two separate colours, Tinta white and a coloured Tinta. The major part of the brushstroke will be white, but the tip will be coloured. The technique also gives a nice effect on other types of small flowers such as for-get-me-not.

When using this technique the flowers are not traced, but painted while the Pergamano parchment paper is still attached to the pattern.

How to load the brush:

Place a drop of white Tinta ink and a coloured ink separately on the palette. First the pointed dry brush is filled with white ink. This is done by horizontally rolling the brush around its own centre in the outer part of the colour. In this way the white colour is mainly on the outside of the brush. Then the tip of the brush is loaded with the coloured ink. When painting very small flowers, only the tip of the longest hair in the brush is filled. To be able to take that little amount of colour out of a drop, it is normally easier if some of the colour is spread out flat on the palette. The brush is then loaded from the spread out coloured ink. Do not leave the tip too long time in the colour, otherwise the coloured ink will mix with the white.

The brush will need to be cleaned before it can be re-loaded.

If the brush is to be loaded with Tinta white first and then with Tinta violet, it will normally appear like this in the painting instructions: Tinta white 01T + violet 07T.

How to hold the brush:

Place the finger about 11 centimetres from the point of the brush.

Position of the brush:

During the work the brush is held horizontally. The brush movement:

The brush is placed down on to the parchment and quickly lifted up again (to dab) so the brush leaves a thin long white brushstroke with a coloured point. Several brushstrokes may be made before it is necessary to load the brush again.

Example B: Heart

Tracing:

Tinta leaf green 10T: The leaves.
Tinta gold 22T: The outlines of the heart.
Tinta white 01T: The lines leading to the folding line.

Colour guide for painting:
Tinta white 01T + violet 07T: The petals of the flowers.
Tinta violet 07T: Shades between the petals.
Tinta yellow 16T: Flower hearts.
Tinta red 03T: Stamens.
Tinta green 04T: The leaves.
Tinta leaf green10T: Shades in the leaves.

Painting instructions:

1. Keep the Pergamano parchment paper attached to the pattern. Load the brush with white Tinta ink and a little violet on the tip. Start dabbing small brushstrokes on the left side of a petal. The tip of the brush touches the outline of the petal and the brushstrokes must follow the natural shape of the petal. Dab the strokes close together going towards the right, so the outer part if the petal is covered with ink. The rest of the petal will eventually be embossed white. Do not make the top flowers too violet .

2. With a pointed brush a small dot of violet Tinta ink painted between the lower part of the petals.

3. Paint the flower centres with yellow Tinta. When the yellow is dry, make a dot in the centre with red Tinta ink.

4. Remove the Pergamano parchment paper from the pattern. Paint the leaves with green Tinta ink using a flat brush. When the green ink is dry, then paint the large leaves again with leaf green Tinta to make them darker.

Dorsing:

Dorso red (ass. 2): The space between the inner heart shaped by the flowers/leaves and the gold outline.

Perforating:

Perforate the four-hole combinations gently with the 4-needle tool.

Embossing:
Emboss the petals and flower centres with the large and small ball embossing tools. The dots between the four-hole combinations and the gold ornaments should be embossed with the extra fine tool. Gently emboss the leaves with the large ball tool.

Cutting:
Re-perforate the four-hole combinations again and cut them into crosses.

Finishing off:
Fold the card and insert a coloured paper of your own choice. Perforate as indicated on the pattern. Take care around the folding lines! Remove the excess paper.

PATTERN B: HEART

1. Dabbing: Tinta white + violet.

2. Applying shadow with Tinta violet.

3. Applying Tinta red.

4. Applying shadow with Tinta leaf green.

Technique: Painting with drop shaped brushstrokes

An important brush stroke to use is the one that leaves you with a drop shape on the parchment. If you are a china painter, this is one of the brush strokes that you have to practice before painting any designs. The brush strokes are ideal for making chrysanthemum petals.

How to load the brush:

One colour painting:

Place a drop of ink on the palette. Place the point of a clean dry brush in the outer edge of the drop. Move the brush gently from side to side so the hairs spread out a little. Now and then role the brush and repeat the side to side movement. The brush is held as horizontally as possible so the hairs are straight. Adjust the loading of the brush to fit the size of the area to be painted.

Gently press the tip of the brush on the palette to the make the brush pointed again.

Two colour painting:
Place a drop of white Tinta and a drop of colour separately on to the palette. First the pointed dry brush is loaded with white ink. This is done by horizontally rolling the brush around its own centre in the outer part of the colour, the tip of the brush is loaded with the coloured ink. Do not leave the tip too long in the colour otherwise the coloured ink will mix too much with the white. The brush has to be cleaned before it can be re-filled.

How to hold the brush:
Hold the brush above the metal where the wooden handle begins.

Position of the brush:
During the work the brush is held at an angle of 45 to 90 degrees.

The brush movement:
Place the pointed brush on the parchment paper and press it down so the hairs spread out. Slowly pull the brush towards you while lifting so the brushstroke ends in a point. In brief, the brush movement is "press and lift".

Wide areas:
If the area is wider than one stroke of the brush, more brushstrokes can be added. If you are right handed, you start painting on the left side. While the first brushstroke is still wet a new one is painted on top of the right side of the first brushstroke. Continue this until the whole area is covered.

Tips:
If the brush is too full, the brushstroke will end with a small drop of paint. If this happens, immediately remove the excess paint with a dry brush.

Technique: Pushing the colour
This technique is often used for shading. It is important that the shading blends in well with the first coat of colour. To enhance the shading, the brush can be pushed sideways to leave a brushstroke that is darker on the one side.

How to load the brush:
As in the previous chapter the brush can be fully loaded with paint or alternatively merely rolled in the paint in order to have paint on the outside only.

How to hold the brush:
Hold the brush above the metal where the wooden handle begins.
Position of the brush:
During the work the brush is held at an angle of about 45 degrees.

The brush movement:
Place the pointed brush on the paper with the brush pointing to the left. Pull the brush sideways down towards you while pressing the brush on the parchment paper. When the movement is correctly done the brushstroke is dark on the left side, with less colour to the right. When painting, it is important that the point of the brush follows the edge of the heavy shadow.

Technique: Fine lines
Thin lines are used for fine details and for accentuating veins in leaves and petals.

How to fill the brush:
As in the previous chapters the brush can be fully loaded with paint or rolled in the paint in order to have paint on the outside only. When making extremely thin lines it is important that the brush contains very little paint.

How to hold the brush:
Hold the brush above the metal where the wooden handle begins.

Position of the brush:
During the work the brush is held at an angle of about 90 degrees.

The brush movement:
Place the pointed brush on to the parchment paper, pressing it gently so the tip of the hairs spread out. Slowly pull the brush towards you while lifting it so the brushstroke ends in a fine point.

Example C: Chrysanthemum
Tracing:
Tinta white 01T: Petals.

Tinta sepia 12T: The flower centres.

Tinta leafgreen 10T: The leaves.

Tinta blue 02T: The curved outline.

Tinta gold 22T: The drop shaped figures in the edge.

White colour pencil: The straight outlines.

Colour guide for painting:
Mix Tinta green 04T + leafgreen 10T: The chrysanthemum leaves.

Mix Tinta leafgreen 10T + blue 02T: Shades and veins in the chrysanthemum leaves.

Mix Tinta green 04T + blue 02T: The blades of grass and some shades.

Tinta blue 02T: More shades on the blades of grass.

Tinta white 01T + blue 02T: The petals.

Tinta blue 02T: A few shades close to the centre of the flowers.

Mix Tinta yellow 16T + red 03T: The centre of the flowers.

Painting instructions:
1: Mix green Tinta ink + leaf green. Paint the chrysanthemum leaves with a flat brush starting from the outer edge. Follow the side veins and paint towards the centre vein. Paint the small spaces between the flowers. Mix leaf green Tinta ink + blue. Paint the shading in the leaves. This is done by pushing the colour towards the outer edge of the leaves on some parts of the leaves. Press the brush hard on to the paper so the colour is graduated and the shading between the first coat and the shadow is as gentle as possible. To give the leaves some shape, you can try shading towards one side of the veins. Use the coloured picture as a guide as to where to shade the leaves. On large leaves like these one coat of the shading colour is normally not sufficient. Try three or four coats of colour, remembering to let the paper dry before painting a new coat of dark green.

2: Mix leaf green Tinta + blue. Accentuate the veins by painting thin lines on the veins with a pointed brush. Start from the inside going towards the outside of the leaves.

3: Mix Tinta green + blue. Paint the blades of grass with a flat brush. Make some shades with the same colour by pressing the colour towards the edges of the leaves. Make some darker shades with Tinta blue.

4: Place a drop of white Tinta ink and blue separately on the palette. Load the brush with white and the tip with blue. Make one or two brushstrokes on each petal starting from the outside going towards the centre. It is OK if fine lines appear in the brush-strokes as it will accentuate the shape of the petals. Make the top flower appear more white than the bottom flowers. Try to make the lower petals more blue than the petals laying on the top. If a dark brushstroke is needed, hold the brush a bit longer in the blue colour. Finally make a few lines or small spots with blue Tinta between the lower part of the petals.

4: Mix yellow Tinta + red to make a warm orange. Fill the flower centres with a flat brush. When dry, press out a shadow along the outline of the centre where the stamens are traced.

Perforating:
Perforate the grid softly with the 5-needle tool.

Embossing:
Emboss the top petals and the centres strongly with the large ball tool. With the reverse end of the tool the leaves are embossed lightly.

Circles are embossed around the centre hole of each 5-needle perforation with the extra fine ball tool. Emboss a line on the inner side of each blue traced curve, then emboss the gold drop shaped figures.

Perforating:
Perforate the 5-needle perforations again, but this time deeper. All the perforations are given a twist with the 5-needle except for the centre perforations in the groups

Finishing off:
Fold the card and insert a coloured paper of your own choice. Perforate along the curved line with

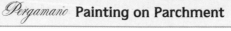

the 2-needle tool. Cut the straight edges with a hobby knife and remove the excess paper.

Technique: Painting with pointed brushstrokes

This is to create a brush stroke that starts and ends with a point. To create fringed or jagged petals, several of these brush strokes are required.

How to fill the brush:

Place drops of white and coloured Tinta inks separately on to the palette. To load the brush with coloured ink, horizintally roll the brush around its own centre in the outer part of the colour. The tip is then loaded by dipping it into the white ink. The brush is now ready for the first brush stroke. Before making a second stroke, the tip has to be filled with white again. Clean and dry the brush before loading it again with the two colours.

If using fuchsia and white Tinta inks, it will normally be written thus: Tinta fuchsia + white.

How to hold the brush:

Hold the brush above the metal where the wooden handle begins.

Position of the brush:

During the work the brush is held in a vertical position.

The brush movement:

The start of the brush stroke is made with the point of the brush. The brush is pressed down so that the hairs spread and the brush stroke becomes wider and the coloured ink now appears on the paper. Finally lift the brush slowly while still pulling the brush towards you, so the brush stroke ends in a point.

Wide areas.
If the area is wider than one stroke of the brush, more brush strokes can be added. Start painting in the left side of the petal. After the first brush stroke, the second stroke is placed 1 - 2 mm to the right of the first stroke. The points of the brush strokes must not touch. but when the hairs spread out, the brush stroke must cover the right half of the previous stroke. The brush strokes must overlap, except for the points.

Technique: Pressing the colour outwards

This technique works well when working with 2 inks on the brush, for example, when creating leaves. It allows the darkest colour to separate out, and it is therefore pressed towards the outer edge. The design is not normally traced when using this technique.

How to fill the brush:

Place drops of black and coloured inks separately on the palette. Horizontally roll the brush around its own centre in the outer part of the coloured ink. Then load the point of the brush by dipping it into a thin layer of the black ink. Be careful with the black ink, it is an extremely strong colour, and it is easy to use too much.

How to hold the brush:

Grasp the brush 11centimetres back from the tip.

Position of the brush:

Hold the brush at an angle of about 30 degrees from the paper.

The brush movement:

Place the brush on the paper with the brush pointing to the left and pull the brush down towards you. When the movement is correctly done the brush stroke is dark on the left, and lighter on the right. When painting, it is important that the point of the brush defines the heavy lines. Keep moving the brush back and forwards until you see that the black colour has spread towards the left edge.

Example D: Carnations

Tracing:
White colour pencil: The outlines.

Colour guide for painting:
Dark fuchsia (Tinta fuchsia 20T + black 11T) + white Tinta 01T: The petals.
Tinta yellow 16T: The flower hearts.
Tinta green 04T + black 11T: The leaves and stalks.

Painting instructions:
1: Keep the design under the Pergamano parchment paper. Mix fuchsia Tinta with a little black ink. Place a drop of white Tinta ink on to the palette. First load the brush with the dark fuchsia and the tip with white. Start painting the left side of a petal. Place the tip of the brush on the outer point of the petal creating a 1-2 mm long fine line with the point of the brush.
2: Press the brush so the hairs spread and the dark fuchsia colour appears on the paper. Pull the brush slowly towards you.
3: Start lifting the brush whilst pulling it towards you. The brush stroke must end with a fine point just outside the flower centre. Dip the tip of the brush in white ink and paint the next stroke 1 mm to the right of the first one. This procedure should be repeated until there is not any coloured paint left in the brush. Clean and dry the brush before filling it again with the two colours. Paint all the petals in this way.
4: Paint a little yellow Tinta in the flower centres using the pointed brush.
Place drops of green and black Tinta ink separately on to the palette. Spread the black ink out on the palette so that it is possible to get a small amount of paint on the brush. Load the brush with green ink and just a tiny bit of black on the tip. Place the brush on the side you want the shading then pull the brush sideways down towards you whilst pressing the brush on to the paper.
5: Keep the brush moving back and forwards until you see the black colour separate out. With the paint that is left in the brush, paint the right side of the leaf and also the stalk. Paint all the leaves in this way. Keep the shading on the same side throughout the design and then take the parchment paper away from the design and check the leaves and stalks for missing outlines.

Embossing:
Emboss the petals strongly with the large ball embossing tool. Emboss the leaves softly with the same tool. Use the extra fine ball to emboss the flower hearts.

Finishing off:
Fold the card and insert a coloured paper of you own choice. Cut the outlines with a hobby knife and remove the excess paper.

PATTERN C: CHRYSANTHEMUM

1. Applying shadow with a mixture of Tinta leaf green + blue.

2. Applying veins with a mixture of Tinta leaf green + blue.

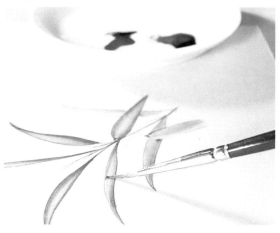

3. Applying shadow with Tinta blue.

4. Painting petals with Tinta white + blue.

5. Applying shadow in the flower hearts with a mixture of Tinta yellow + red.

PATTERN D: CARNATIONS

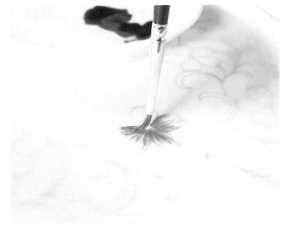

1. Mixture of Tinta fuchsia + black + a tiny bit of white; white comes of the brush first.

2. Mixture of fuchsia + a tiny bit of white: fuchsia comes first of the brush.

3. Fuchsia brush + a tiny bit of white. The end of the brush stroke.

4. Tinta green + black: the beginning of painting the leaves: draw the brush towards you...

5. Tinta green + black:... make pushing movement with the brush.

Example E: Blue landscape

Monochrome painting

To achieve good results in a monochrome painting it is important that the depth of colour varies as much as possible. In this way colour perspective is achieved as in the blue landscape example shown. The example is painted with Tinta ink. As the ink is transparent, so the darkest shades of colour are made up of several coats, (up to 5-6 in the darkest areas). It is important that the ink is allowed to dry completely between each coat, other-wise the paper will become too wet.

Tracing:

Blue Tinta 02T: The whole design.

Colour guide for painting:

Blue Tinta 02T: Landscape, the border between the double outlines.

Painting instructions:

1: Apply a wash of blue Tinta on to the cliff to the left, then paint the two trees. Apply a further wash of blue ink on the hill side. Dilute the blue ink with a little water and paint the foremost mountain. Paint with the same shade the lower part of the water. Dilute the colour even more and paint the mountain in the back ground. Let the ink dry.

2: Apply a coat of blue ink on the cliff and trees to the left of the card. Paint the right

foreground and trees. Paint some shadows in the lower part of the water, and paint the reflections of the trees. Let the blue ink dry.

3: Darken the cliff and the trees to the left with blue Tinta. Remember that to achieve the depth of colour, 5-6 coats of paint must be applied.. When the last coat has dried, stand back, and look at the painting as a whole. At this point some adjustments to the colour effects are still possible.

4: The area between the double outlines are painted with varying shades of blue Tinta. Different parts of the flower design have a differing number of coats of ink. The spaces between the curls should be given two appli-

cations of ink. Study the colour picture carefully before painting.

Embossing:
Use the Hockey Stick to emboss the top outline of the mountains and also the water. Gently emboss the trees on the right with the large ball tool. Emboss between the double outlines with the small and extra fine ball tool. Gently emboss the darkest part in the flower shapes.

Finishing off:
Fold the card and insert a coloured paper of your own choice. Perforate the outlines with the 2-needle tool and remove excess paper.

PATTERN E: BLUE LANDSCAPE

1. First layer of Tinta blue.

2. Second layer of Tinta blue.

3. The painting is ready

4. One of the corner decorations.

TINTA AND PINTURA PAINT

Pintura paints are quick drying water based acrylic paints with a rather thick consistency and they require a moist brush when painting. To achieve the best results, Pintura paints should be used sparingly. They have a glossy appearance.

Painting with PINTURA:

The acrylic paint can separate in the bottle when left, so shake the bottle well before use.

Because the Pintura paint is quick drying only a small drop of colour is placed on the palette.

To achieve a moist brush with the right quantity of water, it is an advantage to use the Pergamano sponge. After the brush has been cleaned in water, it is then dried on the damp sponge. The moist brush is now ready to be filled with Pintura paint.

All the previous painting techniques can be used when painting with Pintura, but it is important that the paint is used sparingly to achieve a more transparent effect. If the Pintura paint is applied too thickly, it will have a streaky, lumpy and sticky surface.

IMPORTANT:

Clean the brush thoroughly immediately after using the Pintura paint. If the Pintura is allowed to dry in the brush it will be ruined, so take care of your brushes.

Tip:

Pintura paint sticks to the surface of the paper rather than soaks down into it, it is easily removed with the Pergamano ink eraser.

PINTURA paint in combined with Tinta ink

In the following examples Tinta ink will be used with Pintura paint. The first layer will be Tinta, because Tinta is easier to paint with when painting larger areas. The shading will be made using Pintura paint because the acrylic paint is less transparent and gives more depth of colour in just the one coat.

Example F: Christmas dog

Tracing:

Tinta black 11T: Eyes, nose and mouth.
Tinta sepia 12T: The rest of the design except for the dots between the perforations.
White colour pencil: The cards outlines.

Colour guide for painting:

Tinta sepia 12T: The dog.
Tinta black 11T: The eyes, nose, mouth and the nail.
Tinta yellow 16T: Every second stripe in the sock.
Tinta green 10T: Every second stripe in the sock and the tip of the sock. The leaves.
Mix Tinta green 10T + blue 02T: The rest of the sock.
Tinta red 03T: The bow, berries and the hearts (not the centre of the hearts with double outlines).
Pintura brown 12: Shades and hairs on the dog.
Pintura yellow ochre 05: Shades in the yellow stripes.
Pintura green 08: Shades on the sock and in leaves.
Pintura red 03: Shades in bow, berries and hearts.

Painting instructions:

1: Paint the dog using sepia Tinta ink, using a flat brush. The eyes and the nose should be given one or two coats of black Tinta. Remember to leave the areas of reflected highlights white.
2: Using brown Pintura paint, build up the required depth of colour of the fur except for the areas around the mouth, nose and eyes. Paint fine hairs with a pointed brush. Make short extra fine hairs on the head and long wavy hairs on the ears.
3: Paint the leaves with a flat brush using green Tinta. The berries and the outside hearts in red Tinta
4: Accentuate the hearts and each berry with

red Pintura. Do not put too much colour on the brush when you paint the berries. Use green Pintura for shading the leaves. Shade half of each leaf, and then accentuate the veins on the other half of the leaf. Look at the photo to see which side of the leaves to shade.

5: Paint the nail with Tinta black (not too heavy).

Paint the bow with a flat brush using red Tinta. Use yellow Tinta to paint each alternate stripe in the sock. The remainder of the stripes and the toe are painted with green Tinta. Mix green and blue Tinta together for the remaining part of the sock. The yellow stripes are shaded with Pintura yellow ochre. Shade along the outlines. Green Pintura is used for shadow on the rest of the sock. Create shadow under the dogs mouth and also under the folded top of the sock. Shade the inside of the bow with red Pintura. Add appropriate shading as per the picture example.

Tracing:
Tinta gold 22T: The hearts and outlines of the gift tag.

Dorsing:
The area behind the dog that is to be dorsed should be masked out with tape to prevent the perforations from being impregnated with the Dorso colour.

To achieve a very soft fusing colour the dorsing process is done twice.

First coat:
Dorso lilac (ass. 2): Dorso the complete square. Finish the process by removing the excess colour with a nylon stocking.

Second coat:
Dorso violet (ass. 1): The lower part of the square.
Dorso pink (ass. 1): The middle part of the square.
Dorso blue (ass. 1): The top part of the square.
Smooth out the Dorso.
Remove the tape carefully. If dark Dorso lines appear on the edges, these can gently be removed with the nylon stocking.
Wipe away the Dorso behind the gift tag with the Pergamano ink eraser. To make the gift tag appear more white it is coloured using the white pencil (on reverse side).

Perforating:
Perforate softly with the 4-needle tool as indicated on the pattern.

Embossing:
Reverse end of tool and large embossing ball: Folded part of sock; ears and the area around the mouth and nose of the dog.
The large embossing tool: The bow and also the leaves between the veins.
Small embossing tool: The eyes; nose; nail; berries; small hearts and also the line inside the hearts which have double outlines.
The extra fine embossing tool: The dots between the perforations.

Cutting:
Perforate the four hole combinations again and cut them into slits.

Finishing off:
Fold the card carefully because of the slits close to the folding line. Insert a coloured paper of your own choice. Cut along the outlines and remove the excess paper.

PATTERN F: CHRISTMAS DOGGIE

1. Tinta ink applied

2. Painted the hairs

3. Tinta ink applied

4. Applying shadow on the leaves with Pintura green.

5. The result.

Example G: Dresden flowers

General information about Dresden Flowers:

Dresden Flowers have a simplified rather than realistic design. In order to give them more shape, it is important to highlight and shade in the appropriate places.

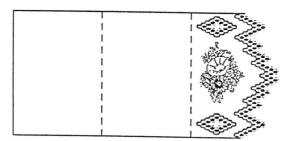

General information about the card:

This card is an envelope card with two folding lines. The perforations are on the front cover and form its outline.

Tracing:

Tinta violet 07T: Morning glory.
Tinta red 03T: Marguerites.
Tinta blue 02T: For-get-me-not.
Tinta sepia 12T: Stamens in Morning Glory.
Tinta leaf green 10T: Leaves and stalks.
Tinta gold 22T: The curved lines.
White pencil: The folding lines and the outlines of the card.

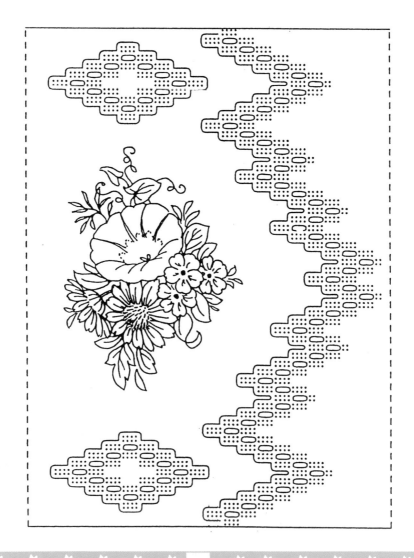

Colour guide for painting:

Tinta violet 07T: Morning Glory.
Pintura violet 07: Shading and veins in the Morning Glory.
Tinta red 03T: Marguerites.
Pintura red 03: Veins in Marguerites.
Tinta blue 02T: Forget-me-not.
Pintura blue 02: Veins in Forget-me-not.
Tinta yellow 16T: Flower centres.
Mix Tinta blue 02T + sepia 12T: Shade in the flower centres of the Morning Glory.
Tinta sepia 12T: Shades in flower centres of the Marguerite and the stamens in the Morning Glory.
Pintura brown 12: Shade in the stamens of the Morning Glory, Marguerite and Forget-me-not.
Mix Tinta green 04T + blue 02T: A few leaves and the blades of grass.
Tinta green 04T: The rest of the leaves and the stalks.
Pintura green 08: Basic shading in the leaves.
Mix Pintura green 08 + blue 02: Darker shading and veins in leaves.

Painting instructions:

1: The Morning Glory is painted with 4 - 5 layers of Tinta violet. Starting in the dark area as specified on the picture, and using a flat brush, commence from the outside and work towards the centre. Follow the natural direction of the petals so that the brush marks will accentuate the shape of the flower. When working towards the highlighted area, add more water to the ink. Be careful not to make the paper too wet. Let the ink dry.

2: Repeat the process above, but using less Tinta violet on the brush. Let the second coat dry before painting the next. Continue to add more coats of colour to the dark area until the desired shade is achieved. Each time a new coat of Tinta violet is added, a smaller area is painted.

3: To add more depth to the colour of the flower we now use the violet Pintura paint. Apply fine lines in the petals going from the inside and working out Accentuate the traced veins with Pintura violet.

The 'trumpet' of the Morning Glory is very pale yellow, so mix yellow Tinta with a lot of water before painting. Mix blue and sepia Tinta on a palette to form a bluish grey colour. Paint fine lines in the 'trumpet' following the natural direction of the flower. The top part should have the darkest shade. Paint the stamens with sepia Tinta and shade them with Pintura brown on one side.

4: The basic colour for the Forget-me-not is blue Tinta. Paint one coat of colour in the dark parts of the lowest flowers. Use less paint on the brush when painting the highlighted areas. Dilute the blue with a little when painting the top flower. Let the ink dry.

5: Paint 3-4 more coats on the Forget-me-not with blue Tinta ink. Use less paint on the top flower and give the lowest flowers the darker shades.

6: Paint fine veins in the Forget-me-not with blue Pintura paint. Paint the flower centre with yellow Tinta ink. Shade the centre with a little brown. Pintura paint.

7: Red Tinta ink is used for the Marguerites. As for the other flowers, the Marguerites also are built up with 4 or 5 coats of ink. Accentuate the veins with red Pintura paint. The basic colour of the flower centres are yellow, so use yellow Tinta but create a soft shadow using sepia Tinta ink before making stamens with brown Pintura paint. Mix a bluish green colour on the palette using green + blue Tinta inks. Paint a few leaves and the blades of grass with this colour. The rest of the leaves and the stalks should be painted with green Tinta. The leaves should be painted with green Pintura. Use the 'pushing' movement with the brush. Mix some green + a little blue Pintura paint and apply shadow to the lowest leaves. Finally make veins in the leaves using the same colour.

Dorsing:

Dorso violet (ass. 1): The area of the perforations.

Perforating:
Perforate the four hole combinations gently.

Embossing:
The large embossing ball: The petals of the Morning Glory, Marguerites and Forget-me-nots. The flower centres of the Marguerite and Forget-me-nots and between the veins on the leaves.

The extra fine embossing ball: Emboss the oblong figures between the perforations. From the front side, fine lines are embossed in the lower part of the 'trumpet' of the Morning Glory.

Cutting:
Perforate the four hole combinations again and cut them into crosses and slits. Cut away the excess paper in the centre of the two squares and along the outline.

Finishing off:
Fold the card and insert a coloured paper of your own choice. Cut off the excess paper.

PATTERN G: 'DRESDEN FLOWERS'

1. First layer with Tinta violet.

2. After 5 layers of Tinta violet.

3. The shadow on the patels and in the flower hart.

4. The first layer of Tinta blue.

5. *After 5 layers of Tinta blue.*

6. *The flower hearts in Tinta yellow with a shadow of Pintura brown.*

7. *The result.*

PINTA-PERLA

Pinta-Perla are waterbased acrylic colours with a mother-of-pearl sheen. They have a glossy appearance and can be mixed with Pintura. They give a soft pastel colouring, except for the bronze Pinta-Perla which becaise it is based on metal pigments, gives a metallic finish.
The Pinta-Perla colours tend to separate in the bottle when left for a while, so shake the bottle before use.

Technique: Circle movement

It can be very difficult to paint with normal brushstrokes when colouring with the acrylic paints, therefore to assist with the application of this paint the circular movement has been devised. With this technique, the colour can be spread out very thinly and in the same movement one can achieve shading.

How to fill the brush:

To achieve a moist brush with the right quantity of water, it is advantageous to use the Pergamano sponge. After the brush has been cleaned in water, it is then dried on the damp sponge. The moist brush is now ready to be filled with Pintura or Pinta-Perla.

One colour in the brush:
Place a drop of Pintura or Pinta-Perla on the palette. load the brush by rolling it horizontally around its own centre in the outer part of the colour.

Two colours in the brush:
Place drops of two different colours of Pintura and/or Pinta-Perla paints separately on to the palette. First load the brush with the base colour, usually the one closest to the centre of the object. This is done by rolling the brush horizontally around its own centre in the outer part of the colour. The second colour is the one that is going to be closest to the outline of the object. Only the tip of the brush to touch the paint for this second colour.
If the brush is first loaded with yellow Pintura paint, then the tip of the brush with Pintura red, it would be written like this: Pintura yellow + a little red.

Three colours on the brush:
Place drops of three different colours of Pintura and/or Pinta-Perla separately on to the palette. First fill the brush with the colour that is to be closest to the centre of the object. This is done by rolling the brush horizontally around its own centre in the outer part of the colour. The next colour is also loaded in the brush with the rolling movement, but a smaller part of the brush is used. The third colour is the one that is going to be closest to the outline of the object. Only the tip of the brush is filled with this colour.
If the brush first is filled with Pintura yellow, secondly with Pintura green and the tip of the brush with Pintura brown, it is normally written like this: Pintura yellow + green + a little brown.

How to hold the brush:
Place the finger about 11 centimetres from the point of the brush.

Position of the brush:
During the work the brush is held at an angle of about 30 degrees from the paper.

The brush movement:
Before starting the actual circular movement the first 6-7 mm is painted so that the colour is pressed towards the outline. By doing this the main part of the colour is gently forced in front of the brush, it can therefore then be spread out on the rest of the design.
Place the pointed brush on the paper and with the brush pointing to the left, pull the brush sideways 6 mm down towards you whilst pressing the brush gently on the parchment paper. When the movement is correctly done the brush stroke is dark in the left side and has less colour in the right side. It is important that the point of the brush follows the darker edge of the design. Keep moving the brush back and forth until you see that a main part of the paint is in front of the brush, then start pressing the brush in an anti-clockwise circular movement whilst still pressing the colour in front of the brush.
The above mentioned instruction describes the way to paint, when painting towards your self. Depending on where the darkest colour is required, it is sometimes necessary to paint away from yourself. The paint is still pressed towards the outline. When the colour is in front of the brush in the painting direction the circle movement is done clock wise pressing the colour away from you.

Example H: Bird in apple tree

In general:
The front-page is larger than the back. The back page ends where the twisted edge begins.

Tracing:
Tinta white 01T: The bird, branch, leaves, flowers and outline.
Tinta fuchsia 20T: The twisted decoration.
Tinta gold 22T: The flower like decorations.
Fold the card and tape the back cover to the design.
Tinta white 01T: A line following the side of the twisted edge that turns inside towards the card.

Colour guide for painting:
Pinta-Perla fuchsia 20N: The back of the petals, stamens and the bird.

Painting instructions:

1: With a flat brush a thin coat of Pinta-Perla fuchsia is painted on the back of the petals. With a pointed brush the stamens are painted with the same colour.

2: Pinta-Perla fuchsia is also used for painting the bird. To shape the bird, the colour is painted on with the circular movement. Paint along the outlines of the body, wing and tail. If the colour appears too light, a second coat can be applied. The eye and the bill are also painted with a pointed brush in Pinta-Perla fuchsia.

Dorsing:

Dorso violet (ass. 1): A soft shade mostly under the branch.
Erase the Dorso violet away from the bird with the Pergamano ink eraser.

Embossing:

From the front the flowers are embossed with the extra fine embossing tool. Emboss with a press and lift movement starting from the outside going towards the centre. The rest of the card should be embossed from the reverse side. Start with the back of the flower using the large ball tool. The stamens are embossed with the fine stylus. The leaves are first embossed with the large ball. Use the press and lift movement going from the outside towards the centre vein and follow the natural direction of the leaves. To make the leaves a little whiter, the small ball tool is used along the outline also with the press and lift movement.

The branch is embossed with both the large and small ball tools. The bird is embossed with the reverse end of the tool and given more whiteness with the white pencil.

Emboss the twisted edge with the large and small ball tools. Emboss the flower like figures with the extra fine ball tool.

Perforating:

Perforate inside the twisted edge with the 2-needle tool as indicated on the design. Perforate along the outlines on the front and back pages.

Cutting:

Cut away the excess paper with the Pergamano scissors.

Finishing off:

Fold the card and insert a coloured paper of your own choice.

PATTERN H: BIRD IN APPLE TREE

1. Painting of the flower.

2. Pinta-Perla fuchsia: circular movement.

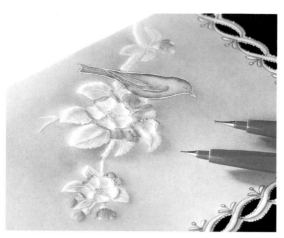

3. The result.

PINTA-PERLA AND PINTURA PAINT

Example I: Baby
Tracing:
Tinta fuchsia 20T: Flower petals.
Tinta sepia 12T: Stamens.
Tinta leafgreen 10T: Leaves.
Tinta red 03T: The baby's bonnet, pillow and quilt.
Tinta gold 22T: The curved lines.
Tinta white 01T: The two small circles.

Colour guide for painting:
Pinta-Perla red 03N: The pillow, every second square in the quilt.
Pintura red 03: The bows on the pillow and the dot on the quilt.
Pinta-Perla yellow + a little Pintura green: The leaves.
Pinta-Perla violet 07N + a little Pintura fuchsia 20: The flowers.
Pinta-Perla light green 04N: The dot in the centre of the flowers.
Mix Pintura white 01 + yellow 16: The stamens.

Painting instructions:
1: Take a little red Pinta-Perla on the brush and paint with circular movements along the outline of every second square in the quilt. Also use the circular movement and red Pinta-Perla for the pillow and its lace. When painting the lace, the tip of the brush should follow the outline of the actual pillow so the outer edge of the lace is left white. When painting the pillow, the tip of the brush should follow the pillows outline and the curved lines under the baby's head.

2. With a little red Pintura on the brush, paint the bow and all the dots in the quilt. The leaves are painted with two colours on the brush and using the circle movement. First the brush is filled with yellow Pinta-Perla and the tip with a little green Pintura. The small leaves at the top of the design are painted by allowing the brush to follow the outline along one side of the leaf. There is normally enough paint to cover the whole area here. The larger leaves are painted in two steps, first the brush follows the outline of the leaf, then to give more shape to the leaf it is necessary to paint along one side of the centre vein.

3: The petals of the flowers are painted with violet Pinta-Perla + a little fuchsia Pintura at the tip of the brush. Start painting with circular movement on one side of the petal and follow the outline all the way round the petal. When all the petals are painted, the centre is given a soft layer of paint.

It is alright to paint over the stamens.

4: Paint the centre dot in the flowers using light green Pinta-Perla. Mix a little white Pintura paint with a tiny amount of yellow on the palette and paint in the stamens using a pointed brush.

Dorsing:

Dorso lilac (ass. 2): The inner space behind the baby.

Smooth out the Dorso.

Dorso red (ass. 2): A little on top of the lilac Dorso.

Smooth out the Dorso.

Erase away the Dorso colour from the bonnet, quilt and pillow.

Perforating:

First perforate gently 4 times with the 5-needle tool in the centre of each perforation group. Then make the four corners with the 3-needle tool. Perforate with the 4-needle tool as indicated on the pattern.

Embossing:

Large and small embossing tool: The white squares in the quilt, the lace on the pillow and the bonnet.

The reverse end of the embossing tool: The actual pillow.

The small embossing tool: The bows and the small dots in the quilts.

Large embossing tool: The flower petals and the

leaves between the veins.

The stylus: A line around the 4 centre holes in the perforation groups.

The extra fine embossing tool: A dot in the corners of the perforation groups and in the four hole combinations. Finally emboss the golden outline.

Perforating:

Perforate again with the 5 and 4-needle tools. Perforate the corners with the 3-needle tool and turn it left and right to make oblong holes.

Cutting:

Cut the centre 4 holes in all the perforation groups into a large cross.

Finishing off:

Fold the card and insert a coloured paper of your own choice. Perforate along the outline and the centre hole as indicated on the pattern. Remove the excess paper. Perforate the two small circles and remove the excess paper. Use the two holes to arrange a red bow (4 mm wide ribbon) on the front side.

PATTERN I: BABY

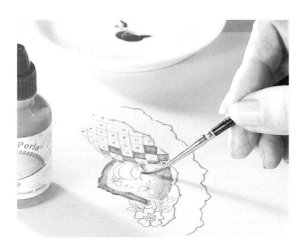

1. Circular movement: Pinta-Perla violet.

2. Pinta-Perla yellow + Pintura green: painting of the leaves.

3. Pinta-Perla violet + Pintura fuchsia: painting of the petals.

4. Close-up of the stamens.

PINTURA PAINT

Example J: Azalea

Tracing:
Tinta red 03T: Flowers and stamens.
Tinta leafgreen 10T: Leaves and stalks.
Tinta gold 22T: The oblong and squared figures between the perforations.
White pencil: The cards outlines.

Colour guide for painting:
Pintura yellow 16 + green 08 + brown 12: The leaves.
Mix Pintura green 08 + brown 12: Veins in leaves.
Pintura green 08: The stalks.
Pintura brown 12: Shading on stalks.
Pintura orange 06 + red 03 + bordeaux 51: The flowers.
Pintura bordeaux 51: Veins in petals.
Pintura violet 07: The stamens.

Painting instruction:
1: Large leaves are painted in four steps, each time covering a quarter of the area. First load the brush with yellow Pintura then green and finally with brown on the tip. Let the tip of the brush point towards the left. Start painting along the outline of the leaf using the circular movement.
2: Clean and load the brush again with yellow + green + brown Pintura. This time paint along the right side of the centre vein, still holding the leaf in the same position.
3: Clean and fill the brush again with yellow + green + brown Pintura. Now turn the leaf 180 degrees and paint along the left outline of the leaf.
4: Clean and fill the brush again and finally paint along the right side of the centre vein. Paint all the large leaves in this way. The smaller leaves are painted by following the outline. Mix green + brown Pintura. Paint fine veins in the leaves with a pointed brush. Paint the stalks with green Pintura and create shading with the brown.

5: The azaleas are painted with orange + red + bordeaux Pintura paint. First the brush is loaded with orange then red, and finally the tip with bordeaux. Point the tip of the brush to the left. Start painting the petal from the centre work out - painting along the left side of the petal and towards yourself. Paint along the outline until there is no more colour remaining on the brush.
6: Clean the brush and load it again with orange + red + bordeaux Pintura. Working again from the centre, paint along the other side of the petal this time painting away from yourself. Paint along the outline until there is no more colour on the brush.
Now paint along one side of the vein starting from the centre of the flower.
Paint the veins with bordeaux Pintura using a pointed brush.
Paint the stamens with violet Pintura.

Dorsing:
Dorso lilac (ass. 2): Behind the flower design.

Perforating:
Perforate gently with the 4-needle tool where indicated on the pattern.

Painting instructions:
7: The 6 oblong spaces between the perforations should be painted on the reverse side of the parchment. First make a fine line along the perforations with Perga-Liner A12. Make the line softer by making circular movements with a moist brush.

Embossing:
Reverse end of tool and the large ball tool: The flower petals and the leaves between the veins.
Stylus: The veins of the leaves, embossed from the front.
The small embossing tool: The gold figures between the perforations.
The extra fine embossing tool: The dots between the perforations.

Cutting:
Perforate again and cut the perforations into crosses and T-shaped figures with the Pergamano scissors.

Finishing off:
Fold the card and insert a coloured paper of your own choice. Cut the outlines with a hobby knife and remove the excess paper.

PATTERN J: AZALEA

1. *Pintura yellow 16 + green 08 + brown 12.*
   Along left side of leaf.

2. *Pintura yellow 16 + green 08 + brown 12.*
   Along left side of vein.

3. *Pintura yellow 16 + green 08 + brown 12.*
   Along right side of leaf.

4. *Pintura yellow 16 + green 08 + brown 12.*
   Along right side of vein.

5. Pintura orange 06 + red 03 + bordeaux 51.

6. Pintura orange 06 + red 03 + bordeaux 51.

7. Softening the Perga-Liner line.

Example K: Girl

General information about painting faces:

Painting faces requires very accurate work specially when tracing. Just a slight deviation in the work, can change the expression and proportions so take time to trace the face very accuratley.

The skin colour is normally applied on the reverse side of the paper to give the skin a matt look with a soft and smooth effect.

Tracing:

Tinta sepia 12T: The face, hair and stamens.
Tinta white 01T: The petals of the flowers, the fur border on the coat.
Tinta red 03T: The hat.

Tinta violet 07T: The feather, ribbon and bow on hat, glove and the rest of the coat.
Tinta leaf green 10T: The leaves and the stalks.
Tinta gold: 22T: The frame around the girl, the frame along the outline, the dots between the perforations.
White pencil: The card outlines.

Colour guide for painting:

Pintura skin colour 13: The face (on the reverse side).
Tinta sepia 12T: The hair.
Mix Pintura cinnamon 51 + a little bordeaux 51: Lines in the hair, eyebrows, eyelashes.
Pintura brown 12: Lines in the hair.
Pintura black 11: The pupils in the eyes.
Mix Pintura blue 02 + white 01: The eyes

(cover the pupil with a thin coat).

Pintura white 01: The white part of the eye.

Pintura bordeaux 51: The hat and the lips.

Pinta-Perla fuchsia 20N + violet 07N: The ribbon, bow and glove.

Pintura violet 07: The feather and lines in the ribbon and bow.

A little Pintura blue 02 + violet 07: The coat (not the fur border).

Pintura fuchsia 20: The petals.

Pintura light green 04: The flower hearts.

Pintura yellow 16 + green 08: The leaves and stalks.

Pintura green 08: Veins in leaves.

Mix Pintura white 01 + a little yellow 16: The stamens.

Tinta gold 22T: The dots between the perforations.

Painting instructions:

1: Paint on the reverse side: The face with Pintura skin colour. Using the circular movement, apply 2/3 thin coats of skin colour.

2: The rest of the design is painted from the front.

Paint the hair with sepia Tinta and follow the direction of the hairs. Mix Pintura cinnamon with a little bordeaux. Paint the eyebrows and laces with very fine lines. Paint fine curved lines in the hair so the hair will look curly.

3: Make more fine lines in the hair with Pintura brown.

The pupils in the eyes should be painted with black Pintura. Mix blue + white to use on the iris and paint a thin coat of this colour over the pupil to prevent the eyes from 'staring'. Paint the rest of the eye white using a thin coat of white Pintura.

4: Bordeaux Pintura is painted on the hat using the circular movement, but do follow the outlines. Paint a little bordeaux Pintura on the lips.

The ribbon, bow and glove are all painted with fuchsia + violet Pinta-Perla. Violet Pintura is used for the feather and some lines in the bow and ribbon.

Take a little blue Pintura and a little violet on the brush and paint the coat (except for the fur border) following the outlines. The circular movement is used to spread the colour.

Use fuchsia Pintura to give the petals a little colour around the centres of the flowers.

Paint the heart with light green Pintura. Mix white with a little yellow Pintura on the palette and paint the stamens.

The leaves and stalks are painted with yellow + green Pintura. The veins should be shaded with green Pintura using a pointed brush.

The dots between the perforations are painted with gold Tinta.

Dorsing:

Reverse side:

Dorso blue (ass. 1): The blue part of the coat.

Dorso violet (ass. 1): The lower horizontal area behind the girl.

Dorso blue (ass. 1): The centre horizontal area behind the girl.

Dorso light blue (ass. 2): The top area behind the girl.

Front side:

Dorso fuchsia (ass. 1): A very little on the cheeks

Perforating:

Perforate gently with the 4-needle tool where indicated on the pattern.

Embossing:

Small ball embossing tool: The curls in the hair and between the veins in the leaves.

Large ball tool: The ribbon, bow and the fingers.

Reverse end of tool: The brim of the hat.

Reverse end of tool and large ball tool: The fur border.

The extra fine ball tool: A small dot in the non grouped four hole combinations. The gold dots.

Embossed from the front side:

Stylus tool: The petals.

Cutting:

Re-perforate and cut out the square shaped groups with the Pergamano scissors.

Finishing off:

Fold the card and insert a coloured paper of your own choice. Cut of the excess paper with a knife.

PATTERN K: GIRL WITH FLOWERS

1. Tracing from the pattern.

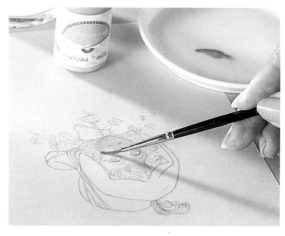

2. Pintura skin colour at the back.

3. The first layer of paint on the hair.

4. The second layer of paint on the hair and the eyes.

5. The result.

MIXING TINTA

The following suggestions are meant as a guide, but many other combinations of colours can also be mixed. Do experiment.

Leaves:
Spring:
First coat: Tinta green 04T + yellow 16T. Tinta green 04T.
Shading: Tinta green 04T. Tinta green 04T + a little blue 02T.

Summer:
First coat: Tinta green 04T. Tinta green 04T + blue.
Shading: Tinta green 04T + a little blue 02T. Tinta green 04T + blue 02T.

Autumn:
First coat: Tinta green 04T. Tinta leaf green 10T.
Shading: Tinta green 04T + blue 02T + sepia 12T. Leaf green 10T + blue 02T + sepia 12T.

Winter:
First coat: Yellow 16T + sepia 12T. Tinta sepia 12T.
Shading: Tinta sepia 12T. Tinta sepia 12T + blue 02T.

Faces:
Tinta white 01T + red +3T + yellow 16T.

Eyes:
Blue:
First coat: Thin coat of Tinta blue 02T.
Shade: Tinta blue 02T.

Brown:
First coat: Thin coat of Tinta sepia 12T.
Shading: Tinta blue 02T + sepia 12T.

Green:
First coat: Thin coat of leaf green 10T + blue 02T.
Shading: Tinta leaf green 10T + blue 02T + sepia 12T.

Grey:
First coat: Thin coat of Tinta blue 02T + sepia 12T.
Shading: Tinta blue 02T + sepia 12T.

Hair:
Black:
First coat: Thin coat of Tinta black 11T.
Shade: Tinta black 11T.

Dark brown:
First coat: Tinta sepia 12T.
Shading: Tinta sepia 12T + black 11T. Tinta sepia 12T + blue 02T.

Light brown:
First coat: Tinta sepia 12T + a little yellow 16T.
Shading: Tinta sepia 12T. Tinta sepia 12T + a little blue 02T.

Blond:
First coat: Thin coat of Tinta yellow.
Shading: Tinta yellow 16T + a little sepia 12T.

Red:
First coat: Tinta sepia 12T + red 03T.
Shading: Tinta sepia 12T. Tina sepia 12T + red 03T.

MIXING PINTURA

The following suggestions are meant as a guide, but many other combinations can be mixed. Do experiment.

Leaves:
Spring:
Pintura light green 04 + green 08.
Pintura light green 04 + blue 02 + brown 12.
Pintura yellow 16 + green 08.
Pintura white 01 + yellow 16 + green 08.
Pintura yellow 16 + light green 04.
Summer:
Pintura green 08 + bordeaux 51.
Pintura green 08 + black 11.
Pintura yellow 16 + green 08 + brown 12.
Pintura light green 04 + blue 02 + brown 12.
Autumn:
Pintura brown 12 + bordeaux 51 + green 08.
Pintura green 08 + bordeaux 51.
Pintura yellow 16 + green 08 + brown 12.
Pintura cinnamon 52 + green 08.
Pintura yellow ochre 05 + green 08.
Pintura orange 06 + green 08 + yellow ochre 05.

Faces:
Pintura skin colour 13.

Eyes:
Light blue:
Pintura blue 02 + turquoise 48 + white 01.

Dark blue:
Pintura blue 02 + violet + brown 12.
Light brown:
Pintura cinnamon 52 + brown 12.
Dark brown:
Pintura black 11 + brown 12.
Light green:
Pintura skin 13 + green 08.
Dark green:
Pintura black 11 + green 08.
Light grey:
Pintura white 01 + blue 02 + brown 12.
Dark grey:
Pintura blue 02 + brown 12.

Hair:
Black:
Pintura black 11 + white 01.
Dark brown:
Pintura orange 05 + brown 12.
Pintura brown 12 + black 11.
Light brown:
Pintura cinnamon 52.
Pintura cinnamon 52 + blue 02.
Blond:
Pintura yellow 16 + yellow ochre 05 + cinnamon 52.
Red:
Pintura yellow ochre 05 + cinnamon 52.
Pintura orange 06 + cinnamon 52.
Pintura orange 06.

PERGA-COLORS

Perga-Colors are waterbased felt-tip pens. They are easy to use and give a matt effect.

When the Perga-Color is applied, there are two ways of spreading out the colour:

1: Using a moist brush.
2: Using a little colour (Pintura or Pinta-Perla) in the brush.

For children, the Pergamano brush no. 2 with the light brown handle is recommended. Adults can use their oldest Pergamano brush no. 2.

Technique: Spreading out with a moist brush

The simplest way of spreading the colour is to use a brush moistened with a little water.

How to apply the PERGA-COLOR

Hold the Perga-Color pen vertically and draw a fine line along the outline of the area that is to be coloured. Hold the work so the line is placed on the right side of the outline. The line should not be more than 2 - 3 cm long because otherwise the paint will dry before it is spread out with the brush. Apply only one layer of Perga-Color. (Two layers will give too much pigment to the paper).

If two Perga-Colors are to be mixed together, the darkest line is normally placed close to the outline. The second line drawn close to the first.

How to fill the brush

Clean the brush in water and dry it on the damp Pergamano sponge.

How to hold the brush:

Place the finger about 11 centimetres from the point of the brush.

Position of the brush:

During the work the brush should be held at an angle of about 30 degrees to the paper.

The brush movement:

Place the brush on the paper with the tip pointing to the left and touching the Perga-Color line (or lines). Start pressing the brush anti-clock wise in small circles into the Perga-Color, forcing the colour in front of the brush and you slowly move it towards you.

When the movement is correctly done the brush-stroke is dark in the left side and has less colour in the right. When painting this way it is important that the point of the brush follows the edge of the heavy shadow.

Technique: Spreading out with colour in the brush

By using an acrylic colour in the brush together with the Perga-Colors give more colour variations and a shinier finish.

How to apply the PERGA-COLOR

Hold the Perga-Color pen vertically and draw a fine line along the outline of the area to be coloured.

If two Perga-Colors are required, two lines should be drawn.

How to fill the brush

Clean the brush in water and dry it on the damp Pergamano sponge. Load you brush a little Pintura or Pinta-Perla by dipping the point if the brush in the paint.

How to hold the brush:

Hold brush about 11 centimetres from the point.

Position of the brush:

Whilst painting, the brush should be held at angle of about 30 degrees to the paper.

The brush movement:

Place the brush on the paper with the brush pointing to the left and the tip touching the Perga-Color line. Start pressing the brush and with the circular movement in an anti-clock wise direction, forcing the colour in front of the brush whilst slowly moving it towards you.

Example L: Ornament with stylised flowers

Tracing:
White pencil: The card outline.
Tinta sepia 12T: The rest of the design.

Colour guide for painting:
Use the coloured picture as a guide.
Perga-Color blue 2: Oblong spaces (8) around the flowers pointing towards the corners.
Perga-Color blue 2 + light green 12: The u-shaped spaces (4) inside the flower circle.
Perga-Color blue 2 + turquoise 9: Oblong spaces (4) outside the centre square.
Perga-Color turquoise 9 + light green 12: The space outside the flower circle.
Perga-Color orange 6: The centre square and the four small squares around it. The small stripes (24), showing the inside of the flowers.

Painting instruction:
In this example all the Perga-Colors are spread out with a moist brush using the circular movements.

1: Blue Perga-Color is used for the oblong figures (8) around the flowers pointing towards the corner. Draw a blue line from top to bottom of one space just beside the outline. Spread it out immediate after with a moist brush. Colour the other areas in the same way.

2: The u-shaped figures (4 in all) are too large to be painted in one go, so divide the space into four parts and paint them individually. First draw a line along the outline with the blue Perga-Color then paint a line with light green Perga-Color 12 just beside it. Mix the two lines together by using the circular movement with a moist brush.
Use the blue + turquoise Perga-Color and draw along the 4 small oblong spaces out-

side the centre square. Outside the flower circle the space should be cloured with turquoise + light green Perga-Color. Colour only 2- 3 centimetres at a time.
Finally, orange Perga-Color is used for the centre square, the 4 small squares around it and the inside of the flower. The latter is seen as two small thin spaces on each flower.

Tracing:
Tinta gold 22T: All lines except for the card outlines.

Perforating:
Perforate gently with the 4-needle tool where indicated.

Embossing:
3: The large ball embossing tool: The flowers petal embossed in three separate parts. Then the centre square.

Small embossing ball: A small square in the 4 larger squares under the flowers. A smaller figure in the lentil shaped figures (8 in all).
Extra fine embossing ball: The drop shaped figures along the outline. A small dot in every second perforation. Start with perforation no. 2, so the first one later can be cut into a cross.

Stippling:
Use the stippling technique on the stamens.

Cutting:
4: Re-perforate and cut every second perforation into a cross with the Pergamano scissors. Start with the perforation farthest out in each group.

Finishing off:
Fold the card and insert a coloured paper of your own choice. Cut along the outline and remove the excess paper.

PATTERN L: PHANTASY CARD

1. Perga-Color bleu 2.

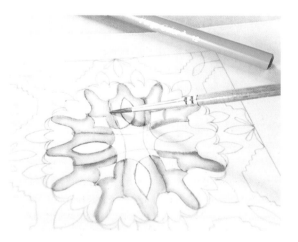

2. Perga-Color bleu 2 + light green 12.
See the result on page 61.

Example M: Jungle

Tracing:
Tinta black 11T: The complete design.

Colour guide for painting:
Perga-Color red 1 and Pintura red 03: The point of the beak, spot on top of tail.

Perga-Color light green 12 and Pintura yellow 16: Rest of the beak.

Perga-Color yellow 3 and Pintura yellow 16: The head of the Toucan.

Tinta black 11T: The rest of the bird.

Pintura black 11: Shadows on the bird.

Perga-Color light green 12, Pintura yellow ochre 05 and Pintura light green 04: The palm leaves.

Perga-Color orange 6 and Pintura orange 06: The oranges.

Perga-Color green 4 and Pintura yellow 16: The orange leaves.

Perga-Color red 1 and Pinta-Perla red 03N: The orchids.

Perga-Color green 4 and Pintura light green 04: The orchid leaves.

Perga-Color brown 5 and Pintura brown 12: The trunk of the palm tree and orange tree.

Perga-Color brown 5 and Pintura light green 04: The vine.

Tinta black 11T: The frame and the centre part of the 4 fans.

Pintura black 11: Shades in frame and the centre parts of the 4 fans.

Perga-Color light green 12 and Pintura light green 04: The outer rectangles of the fans.

Perga-Color orange 6 and Pintura orange 06: The last rectangle in the fans.

Painting instruction:
In this example the Perga-Colors are spread with Pintura or Pinta-Perla in the brush using the circular movements.

1: Draw along the outline of the point of the beak with red Perga-Color. Spread the colour out with red Pintura using circular movements. Colour the spot on the top of the tail in the same way. Apply a few spots of Perga-Color along the outline of the rest of the beak and use yellow Pintura to spread the colour. Paint the head of the bird with yellow Perga-Color and yellow Pintura. Paint a thin coat of black Tinta over the rest of the Toucan. Create shading with the black Pintura using circular movements along the outlines.

2: Paint a palm leaf on the right side of the tree so that the tip of the leaf is pointing up. Aply a line of light green Perga-Color along the left outline and spread it out with yellow ochre. Pintura

3: On the right side of the vein, apply a line with the light green Perga-Color then spread it out with yellow ochre Pintura.

4: Create a turn on the leaf so the tip is pointing down. Use light green Perga-Color along the left outline and spread it out with light green. Pintura. Continuing this action, colour along the right side of the vein with the moist brush to give this part of the leaf a thin coat of colour.
Paint the rest of the Palm Tree leaves in the same way. Place the dark shade in the part of the leaf that turns down.

5: Paint the oranges with orange Perga-Color and orange Pintura. The Orange Tree leaves are painted in two stages. First draw a line with green Perga-Color along the left outline of the leaf and spread it out with yellow Pintura. Draw another line, this time with green Perga-Color on the right side of the vein and spread it out with yellow Pintura.
The orchids are painted with red Perga-Color and red Pinta-Perla. The rest of the leaves are painted with green Perga-Color and light green Pintura.
Use brown Perga-Color and brown Pintura for the trunk of the both the Palm Tree and the Orange Tree. The Vine should be coloured with brown Perga-Color and light green Pintura.
A thin coat of black Tinta is painted on the frames and centre parts of the 4 fans. Shade the areas with the black Pintura using the circular movements along the outlines. Paint the outer rectangle of the fans with light green Perga-Color and light green Pintura. The last rectangle in the fan is painted with orange Perga-Color and orange Pintura.

Tracing:
Tinta gold 22T: The double frame and all details in the fans.

Dorsing:
Dorso blue (ass. 1): The lower part of the back ground.

Dorso light blue (ass. 2): The top part of the back ground.

Embossing:
Reverse end and the large ball embossing tool: The bird, the oranges and the orchids. A soft embossing in all the leaves on both sides of the veins.

Small embossing ball: The rectangles in the fans.

Cutting:
Perforate along the fans with the 2-needle. Cut the connections with the Pergamano scissors.

Finishing off:
Fold the card by embossing the folding line with the extra fine ball tool. Use a ruler as support. Fold the card and insert a coloured paper of your own choice. Cut along the straight outlines through all 4 sheets of paper. Remove the excess paper on the front side. Open the card and cut away the excess paper on the insert and the back page.

PATTERN M: JUNGLE

1. Some spats of Perga-Color light green 12, Pintura yellow 16 on the brush.

2. Perga-Color light green 12 + Pintura yellow ochre 05.

3. Perga-Color light green 12 + Pintura yellow ochre 05.

4. Perga-Color light green 12 + Pintura light green 04.

5. Perga-Color green 4 + Pintura yellow 16.

REPEATING THE TECHNIQUES

Example N: Window hanger

General:
To make this window hanger you need Pergamano stamp PS-1, silver embossing powder, stamping pad and two square passepartouts with an inner hole of 75 x 75 mm.

Rubber stamping:
Make 1 stamp impression on the Pergamano paper. Follow the instructions from the PS-1 package.

Tracing:
Tinta violet 07T: The 6 elements.

Painting:
The stamp impression consists of 8 flower-like figures, 4 large ones in the centre and 4 smaller ones (One in each corner). Use the coloured picture as a guide.
Perga-Color blue 2 + fuchsia 7: The centres of the flowers and the 6 elements.
Perga-Color lilac 11: The space around the small flowers.

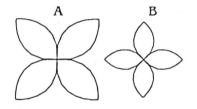

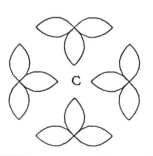

Perga-Color lilac 11 + fuchsia 7: The oblong space between the small flowers.
Perga-Color light green 12: The small squares in top of the flowers.

Tracing:
Tinta silver 21T: The outlines of the elements.

Perforating:
Perforate gently with the 4-needle tool as indicated on the pattern.

Embossing:
Large embossing ball: The centres of the flowers and the elements.
Small embossing ball: The light green squares and the dots between the perforations. Emboss a smaller triangle in the triangular shaped figures of the flowers.

Cutting:
Re-perforate with the 4-needle tool and cut the perforations into crosses.
Perforate along the outlines of the elements and cut away the excess paper.

Embossing:
Large embossing ball: The elements.

Finishing off:
Glue the Pergamano paper and the 2 passepartout cut-outs together.
Use Pergakit to glue the elements to the front page of the window hanger. Place first element A on to the centre and B on top of that. Place the C elements as indicated on the photo.
Pierce a hole in one of the corners of your project. Now insert a nylon thread and hang the decoration in the window.

Example O: Snowman

Tracing:
Tinta red 03T: Skies, the top and bottom of the ski stick.
Tinta black 11T: Hat, eyes, nose, the rest of the ski stick.
Tinta violet 07T: The scarf.
Mix Tinta sepia 12T + blue 02T: The snowman, the snowdrifts.
Tinta leaf green 10T: The trees, the ribbon on the gift.
Tinta sepia 12T: The rest of the gift, the moon.
Tinta white 01T: The card outline.
Tinta silver 21T: The drop shaped figures between the perforations.

Painting:
Pintura orange 06: The ribbon on the hat and the thin stripes in the scarf.
Pintura black 11: The rest of the hat, the eyes, the ski stick.
Pinta-Perla white 01N: The snowman and the snowdrifts in the foreground.
Mix Pinta-Perla white 01N + a little blue 02N: The snowdrifts in the background.
Pintura red 03: The skies, the top and bottom part of the ski stick.
Pintura violet 07: The rest of the scarf.
Pintura light green 04: The ribbon on the gift.
Pintura yellow 16: The moon and the gift.
Pintura green 08: The trees.

Dorsing:
Reverse side:
Dorso violet (ass. 1): The lower part of the sky.
Dorso blue (ass. 1): The centre part of the sky and behind the snowdrifts in the background.
Dorso light blue (ass. 2): The top part of the sky.
Front side:
Dorso fuchsia (ass. 1): A little on the cheeks of the snowman.

Perforating:
Perforate gently with the 4-needle tool as indicated on the pattern.

Embossing:
Hockey-Stick: Along the outlines of the snowman.
Large embossing ball: The hat, the ribbon on the hat and gift, the front of the skies, the top of the ski stick, the nose.
The small ball embossing tool: The eyes, the trees, the ski stick.
The extra fine embossing ball: The orange stripes in the scarf. The dots between the perforations.

Painting:
Reverse side:
White colour pencil: The snowman.

Cutting:
Re-perforate and cut the perforations into crosses. Cut the connections between the outer crosses on the top of the card.

Remove the excess paper from the perforations.

Finishing off:
Fold the card and insert a coloured paper of your own choice. Cut along the complete outline of the card with the 2-needle tool. Remove the excess paper.

Example P: Mushrooms

Tracing:
Tinta white 01T: The stem of the mushrooms and the curved outline.
Tinta leaf green 10T: The leaves.
Mix Tinta yellow 16T + sepia 12T: The cap of the mushroom.
Mix Tinta blue 02T + sepia 12T: The gills of the mushroom.
Tinta gold 22T: The double frame and the small squares between the perforations.
White pencil: The rest of the card outlines.

Painting:
Mix Tinta yellow 16T + a little sepia 12T: The centre of the caps.
Mix Tinta yellow 16T + sepia 12T: The sides of the caps.
Pintura cinnamon 52: Shades and fine lines on the caps.
Mix Tinta blue 02T + sepia 12T (brown grey): The gills and shading on one side of the stems.

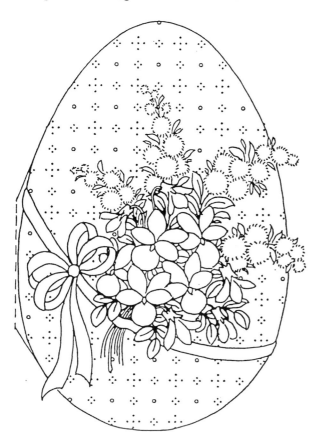

Mix Tinta blue 02T + sepia 12T + a little fuchsia 20T: Shading and fine lines on the gills.
Tinta green 10T: The top of the leaves.
Mix Tinta green 10T + blue 02T: The lower part of the leaves.
Pintura green 08: Shading in the leaves.

Perforating:
Perforate gently with the 4-needle tool as indicated on the pattern.

Embossing:
Hockey-stick and the reverse end of an embossing tool: The caps.
Large embossing ball: The stems, between the double gold lines, the small squares between the perforations. Emboss the leaves softly. Emboss the gills from the front side.
Small embossing tool: The dots between the perforations and the curved outlines.

Cutting:
Re-perforate with the 4-needle tool and cut the perforations into slits.
Perforate with the 2-needle tool and cut away the excess paper between the mushrooms and the leaves.

Finishing off:
Fold the card and insert a coloured paper of your own choice. Perforate along the curved outlines and cut away the rest of the excess paper with a hobby knife.

Example Q: Easter egg

Tracing:
Tinta violet 07T: The violets.
Tinta red 03T: The stamen of the violets.
Mix Tinta yellow 16T + sepia 12T: The mimosas.
Tinta leaf green 10T: The leaves and stalks.
Tinta turquoise 05T: The ribbon.
Tinta white 01T: The outline of the egg.
Tinta gold 22T: The dots between the perforations.

Painting:
Violets:
Mix Tinta turquoise 05T + fuchsia 20T and

make various shades of colour petals. Shade the petals with Pintura violet 07 and make some veins in the 3 lower petals. Paint the stamen with a little Pintura orange 06.

Mimosas:
Paint one coat of Tinta yellow 16T and use Pintura yellow ochre 05 for the shading effects.

Leaves and stalks:
Use Tinta green 04T as the basic colour. Paint shadows and veins with Pintura green 08.

Ribbon:
Load the brush with Pinta-Perla white 01N + Tinta turquoise 05T and shade the areas where applicable. Complete the rest of the ribbon with white Pinta-Perla. And mix Mix turquoise and violet Tinta for the shaded areas. Finally give the ribbon a thin wash of fuchsia Tinta diluted with water.

Perforating:
Perforate gently with the 5 and 4-needle tools as indicated on the pattern.

Embossing:
Reverse end of tool and the large ball embossing tool: The violets and the mimosas.
Large ball tool: Emboss the leaves softly.
Large and small ball tool: The ribbon.
Extra fine ball tool: A dot in the 4-needle perforation. A curved line around the 5-needle perforations. The gold dot.

Perforating:
Re-perforate with the 4-needle and then perforate with the 5-needle. Give the latter perforations a gentle twist so the holes becomes oblong.

Finishing off:
Fold the card and insert a coloured paper of your own choice. Perforate along the outline with the 2-needle tool then cut the perforations with the Pergamano scissors and remove the excess paper.

Example R: Rose

Tracing:
Tinta white 01T: The rose.

Tinta leaf green 10T: The leaves and stalks.
Tinta gold 22T: The curved frame and the dots.
White pencil: The card outlines.

Painting:
Tinta white 01T: The highlights on the rose and buds.
Tinta white 01T + red 03T: The different shades of the rose and buds.
Tinta red 03T: Deep shades and fine lines in rose.
Tinta green 04T: Highlights in the leaves.
Tinta green 04T + blue 02T: The rest of the leaves and the stalks.
Pintura green 08: Shading in leaves.
Pintura green 08 + brown 12: Deep shading in leaves and the veins.
Pintura brown 12: Shading of the stalks.
Pintura violet 07: Shading on the inside of the curved frame.

Perforating:
Perforate gently with the 3 and 7-needle tools as indicated on the pattern.

Dorsing:
Dorso violet (ass. 1): Inside the frame.

Embossing:
Hockey-stick and the large ball embossing tool: The white parts of the rose and buds.
Large embossing ball: Gently between the veins of the leaves. The stalks and green leaves on the buds.
Extra fine embossing tool: Ring around the centre of the 7-needle perforation. Curved line around the 3-needle perforations. The curved frame and the dots.

Perforating:
Re-perforate with the 7 and 3-needle tools. Give the 3-needle tool a twist to create oblong perforations.

Finishing off:
Fold the card and insert a coloured paper of your own choice. Cut away the excess paper.